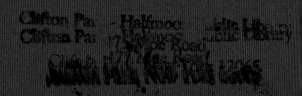

CONSTITUTION DAY

by Robin Nelson

first step nonfiction

x

Lerner Publications Company · Minneapolis

We **celebrate** Constitution
Day every year.

2009			**September**			
SUNDAY	MONDAY	TUESDAY	WEDNESDAY	THURSDAY	FRIDAY	SATURDAY
		1	2	3	4	5
6	7	8	9	10	11	12
13	14	15	16	17 Constitution Day	18	19
20	21	22	23	24	25	26
27	28	29	30			

This holiday is in September.

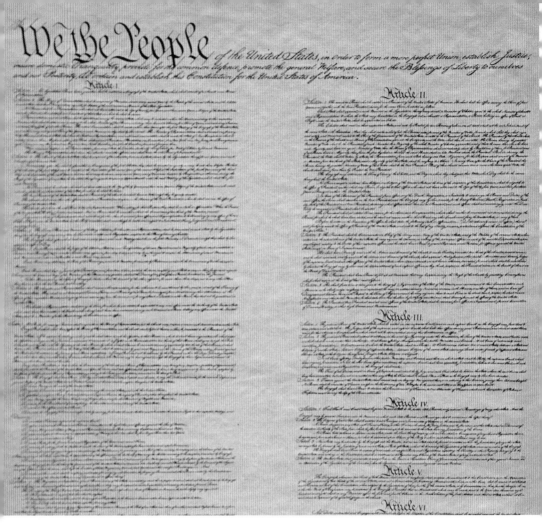

The U.S. **Constitution** is a list of rules.

Our **government** must follow
these rules.

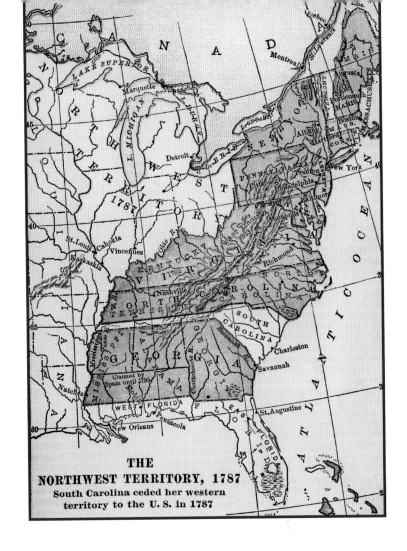

THE
NORTHWEST TERRITORY, 1787
South Carolina ceded her western
territory to the U. S. in 1787

Long ago, the United States of
America was a new **country**.

Many **Americans** met to
write the Constitution.

They wanted our country to
be free.

They wanted people to be
treated fairly.

Executive

Legislative

Judicial

The Constitution split the government into three parts.

All three parts must work together to be fair.

The Constitution was signed
on September 17, 1787.

In 2005, we celebrated the first Constitution Day.

On this holiday, we learn
about the Constitution.

We learn about our country.

On Constitution Day, we celebrate our freedom.

We celebrate being an American.

Constitution Day Timeline

1776
The United States declares that it is free from Great Britain by signing the Declaration of Independence.

September 17, 1787
The U.S. Constitution was signed.

May 25, 1787
Americans began to write the U.S. Constitution.

2005
A law was passed saying that schools should celebrate Constitution Day.

1791
The Bill of Rights is added to the Constitution.

September 16, 2005
The first Constitution Day was celebrated.

Constitution Day Facts

Constitution Day was once called Citizenship Day.

Constitution Day is celebrated by schools each year on September 17. That date could be on a weekend. Then the holiday would be celebrated on the week before or after.

The U.S. Constitution is the oldest written constitution in the world.

The U.S. Constitution has 4,440 words. It is four pages long.

You can see the actual U.S. Constitution in Washington, D.C. It is kept in a bulletproof case that is lowered each night into a vault that has five-ton doors.

The U.S. Constitution was signed by 39 men.

Many important people helped write the U.S. Constitution, including George Washington, Thomas Jefferson, and Benjamin Franklin.

Glossary

 Americans – people who live in the United States of America

 celebrate – to have a party or special activity to honor a special occasion

 constitution – basic rules on how a country should be run

 country – a land where people live under one government

 government – a group of people who lead a country

Index

The images in this book are used with the permission of: AP Photo/South Bend Tribune, Jim Rider, pp. 2, 22 (2nd from top); © Independent Picture Service, p. 3; © Joe Sohm/Visions of America/ Digital Vision/Getty Images, pp. 4, 22 (third from top); © Chip Somodevilla/Getty Images, pp. 5, 10 (bottom left), 22 (5th from top); © North Wind Picture Archives, pp. 6, 8, 9, 22 (4th from top); © SuperStock, Inc./SuperStock, pp. 7, 22 (1st from top); © Xinhua/ZUMA Press, p. 10 (top); AP Photo/J. Scott Applewhite, File, p. 10 (bottom right); © Pablo Martinez Monsivais-Pool/Getty Images, p. 11; *Washington Directs the Signing of the Constitution of the United States, September 17, 1787* by Henry Hintermeister. Gift of the Norden family in memory of Robert Norden, 1965. Collection of Fraunces Tavern® Museum, New York City. (Image provided by SuperStock), p. 12; AP Photo/The Journal of Martinsburg, Martin B. Cherry, p. 13; AP Photo/Bill Wolf, p. 14; © Ted Spiegel/CORBIS, p. 15; © Michael Ventura/Alamy, p. 16; © Jim West/Alamy, p. 17.
Cover: © Alan Crosthwaite/Dreamstime.com.

Lerner Publications Company
A division of Lerner Publishing Group, Inc.
241 First Avenue North
Minneapolis, MN 55401 U.S.A.

Website address: www.lernerbooks.com

Library of Congress Cataloging-in-Publication Data

Nelson, Robin, 1971–
     Constitution Day / by Robin Nelson.
          p.   cm. — (First step nonfiction - American holidays)
     Includes index.
     ISBN 978-0-7613-4930-3 (lib. bdg. : alk. paper)
     1. Constitution Day (U.S.)—Juvenile literature. 2. United States. Constitution—Anniversaries, etc.—Juvenile literature. 3. United States—Politics and government—1783–1789—Juvenile literature. 4. Constitutional history—United States—Juvenile literature. I. Title.
E303.N456 2010
394.263—dc22   2009001865

1848

Manufactured in the United States of America
1 2 3 4 5 6 – DP – 15 14 13 12 11 10